Animal Rights

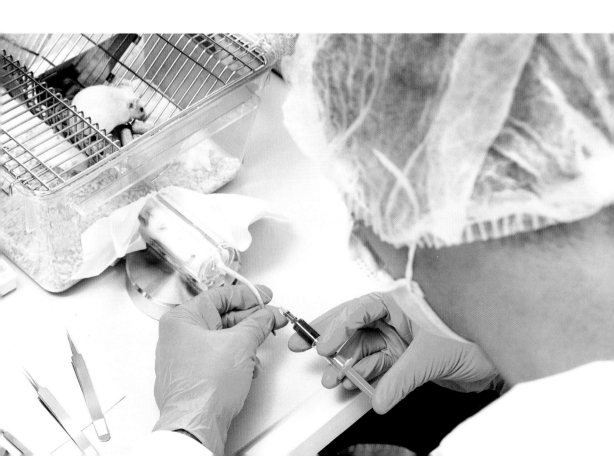

Critical World Issues

Abortion
Animal Rights
The Arms Trade
Capital Punishment
Consumerism
Drugs
Equal Opportunities
Euthanasia

Food Technology
Genetic Engineering
Genocide
Human Rights
Poverty
Racism
Refugees
Terrorism

Animal Rights

Patty Taylor

MASON CREST
PHILADELPHIA

Mason Crest
450 Parkway Drive, Suite D
Broomall, PA 19008
www.masoncrest.com

©2017 by Mason Crest, an imprint of National Highlights, Inc.

Printed and bound in the United States of America.

CPSIA Compliance Information: Batch #CWI2016.
For further information, contact Mason Crest at 1-866-MCP-Book.

First printing
1 3 5 7 9 8 6 4 2

Library of Congress Cataloging-in-Publication Data

   on file at the Library of Congress
      ISBN: 978-1-4222-3647-5 (hc)
      ISBN: 978-1-4222-8127-7 (ebook)

Critical World Issues series ISBN: 978-1-4222-3645-1

Table of Contents

KEY ICONS TO LOOK FOR:

 Words to Understand: These words with their easy-to-understand definitions will increase the reader's understanding of the text, while building vocabulary skills.

 Sidebars: This boxed material within the main text allows readers to build knowledge, gain insights, explore possibilities, and broaden their perspectives by weaving together additional information to provide realistic and holistic perspectives.

 Research Projects: Readers are pointed toward areas of further inquiry connected to each chapter. Suggestions are provided for projects that encourage deeper research and analysis.

 Text-Dependent Questions: These questions send the reader back to the text for more careful attention to the evidence presented there.

 Series Glossary of Key Terms: This back-of-the book glossary contains terminology used throughout this series. Words found here increase the reader's ability to read and comprehend higher-level books and articles in this field.

What Are Animal Rights?

J eff is 19 years old and works at one of Europe's biggest animal research centers. The center experiments on over 70,000 animals every year to help companies all over the world develop drugs and other products for human use.

Jeff explains, "I've always loved animals. Ever since I was little, I've had pets. When I was about eight, my sister and I finally managed to persuade our parents that we could look after a pair of mice; they were great. We've had rabbits, guinea pigs, and cats since then.

"I decided very early on that I wanted to work with animals after I left school, and I always wanted to be a vet. I had a Saturday job at a rescue center looking after horses and ponies that had been mistreated or neglected, and it was amazing see-

Worldwide, millions of animals are experimented on each year to test the possible effects of drugs and other new products, such as cosmetics and household chemicals, on humans and the environment.

ing them getting healthy and starting to trust humans again.

"The animals I look after now are used in experiments to find out if new drugs are safe for humans to use. My friends say I'm crazy to get involved in something like that. They think I'm dosing animals up to the eyeballs with poisons to find out what happens to them, but I'm not. All the experiments are carefully controlled, and we do not use animals unless we absolutely have to. There are laws that say lifesaving drugs cannot be given to humans until they've been tested on animals to make sure they are safe."

Jeff notes that public misunderstandings about how the center where he works treats animals sometimes results in violence. The managing director of the center was once beaten up outside his home by animal-rights activists trying to get the facility closed down. There have been other incidents as well. "Somebody I work with had their car fire-bombed by the animal-rights people. They were sent letters with razor blades taped into them so that they'd cut their fingers when they opened them. Some of the razor blades even had rat poison on them.

"All we're trying to do is help people. My sister has cystic

 Words to Understand in This Chapter

exploit—to make use of cruelly or unfairly for one's own advantage.

speciesism—prejudice or discrimination based on species; especially discrimination from humans against animals.

About 800 marchers defended the use of animals in biomedical research during the UCLA "Pro-Test" campaign in Los Angeles, 2009.

fibrosis, and one of the drugs we're testing at the moment could really be useful to her. Nobody here wants to hurt animals or take unfair advantage of them, and we look after them well. If I thought they were being cruelly treated I'd be the first one to walk."

Jeff's perspective represents just one particular viewpoint on the complex issue of animal rights today. People around the world hold very different views on how humans should treat animals.

Many people believe it is always wrong to experiment on animals. Some try to set them free, while others demonstrate or use violence against people and property in order to get their point across. These demonstrators in Milan, Italy, are protesting against practices at a testing center called Green Hill—in particular, vivisection, or the practice of performing operations on live animals as part of scientific research.

What Are Animal Rights?

Humanity's relationship with the other animal species on Earth is complex. Many people share their homes and their lives with animals, and since the beginning of time, humans have assumed the right to make use of animals for their own benefit.

The Universal Declaration of Human Rights was set out by the United Nations in 1948. It says that people everywhere, no matter who they are, are born free and equal. They have basic rights and freedoms that should be protected by national and international law. In return, they have the responsibility to respect the rights and freedoms of others and to observe the laws and customs of the societies they live in.

Members of animal-rights groups say that like humans, animals also have the right to live freely. They believe that animals' rights—to be free from slavery and ill-treatment—should be protected by national and international law, just as the rights of humans are.

Supporters and Opponents

There are people all over the world who believe that animals should have rights. They say that the Universal Declaration of Human Rights protects humans from being *exploited*, and animals need the same kind of protection. They maintain that animals have the right to not be used to test drugs and other products, killed for their fur, or hunted for pleasure. They are also against some modern farming methods used to raise livestock for people to eat.

Some animal-rights activists use violence against humans

Organizations like People for the Ethical Treatment of Animals (PETA) protest against the use of animal pelts in fashion.

and property in order to make their point, while others may set captive animals free. Many follow the ideas of Peter Singer, a philosopher who said it is wrong to regard animals as inferior to humans. He used the word *speciesism* to describe the way humans discriminate against animals and compared this behavior to racism.

Some people argue that animals do not need rights. Animals, they say, are not as intelligent as humans. Only humans can understand ideas like duty and responsibility and realize that they have to give something back in exchange for the right to live as they choose.

Many humans believe it is acceptable to use animals for their own benefit—receiving lifesaving hospital treatment as a result of tests originally carried out on animals, for example— as long as they look after them properly and treat them kindly.

 # Text-Dependent Questions

1. Identify and explain three different views on how humans should treat animals.
2. What are the rights and responsibilities that people have according to the 1948 Universal Declaration of Human Rights?

 # Research Project

Using the Internet or your school library, do some research on animal rights, and answer the following question: "Should animals have rights?" Some, like Peter Singer, claim all species are equal, and animals should have the same rights and freedoms as humans. Others contend that humans are the most intelligent species, and that animals are an inferior species put on Earth for the benefit of humans. Write a two-page report, using data you have found in your research to support your conclusion, and present it to your class.

Humanity's Relationship with Animals

Humans have had a complicated relationship with animals that has changed over the course of history. Humans and animals need each other in many ways, and their actions have direct and indirect effects on each other.

In prehistoric times, the relationship between humans and other animals was a matter of survival: kill or be killed. Over tens of thousands of years, humans found many uses for animals. Prehistoric humans ate animal flesh, used animal hides for clothing and shelters, and utilized animal bones as crude tools or weapons. Over time they learned that other foodstuffs produced by animals, such as eggs, milk, and honey, tasted good and were nourishing.

Hunting foxes with dogs was part of traditional country life in the United Kingdom. However, as growing numbers of people came to believe that the sport is cruel to animals, most forms of fox hunting have been banned in the United Kingdom since 2005.

Many land-based animals, as well as those that flew or swam, were hunted and killed by humans for their meat and their skins. Other animals were strong and could be used to pull heavy things, frighten enemies, or travel for hundreds of miles without food or water to take valuable goods to those who would pay money for them.

Over time, humans realized they could feed, house, and care for animals conveniently, nearby where they lived, and kill them when they were ready to rather than only when they could catch them. These people started the first farms. They found out that some animals made willing workers, too, and were much less trouble than human ones. Some were quite fun and good to have around, almost like part of the family.

As civilizations and organized religions emerged, some cultures came to believe that Earth and its animals were intended for human use. The Book of Genesis, a book of the Bible considered sacred by Christians and Jews, says that God made man in His own image, and gave him "dominion over the fish of the sea, and over the fowl of the air, and over the cattle, and over every creeping thing that creepeth upon the earth." This thought would become dominant in the western civilizations of Europe for more than 1,500 years.

 Words to Understand in This Chapter

cull—to control the size of a group of animals by killing some of them.

predator—an animal that lives by killing and eating other animals.

It was not until the seventeenth century, when a few influential European philosophers raised questions about whether people had the right to treat animals as they did, that anyone gave a thought to the idea that animals might be anything other than human property. During this decade the first laws were passed to restrict the cruel treatment of certain animals. However, these laws would not become widespread until much later.

Few people now share René Descartes's view that cutting open an animal is no different from sawing a piece of wood.

René Descartes, a French scientist and philosopher who worked in the seventeenth century, conducted experiments on animals to see how similar they were to humans. Descartes came to believe that animals could not experience either pain or pleasure. He concluded that animals did not have either intelligence or emotions.

Evolving Perspectives

When Charles Darwin proposed that humans had evolved over millions of years from an ape-like species like a chimpanzee, people began to wonder whether the planet and everything in it really had been created simply for humanity's benefit. Darwin's theory of evolution, described in *The Origin of Species* (1859), argued that for any species to survive and prosper, it

Charles Darwin once wrote, "Animals, whom we have made our slaves, we do not like to consider our equal." Although not an animal rights activist in the modern sense of the term, Darwin's work did change many people's thinking about animals and humanity's relationship with them.

had to be the best at dealing with all the challenges life threw at it. Darwin called this idea "survival of the fittest."

Maybe early humans had just been better than other animals at protecting themselves against *predators*. Maybe they were just more highly evolved and able to think about things in a different way. For example, they were able to invent weapons and traps—something other animals have not yet evolved the ability to do. It is not hard to understand that humans took power over other animals simply because they could.

Once Darwin suggested that people were simply highly evolved animals themselves, human philosophers, scientists, and religious leaders found themselves with tough questions to answer. Some decided there was no difference between humans and animals, while others remained convinced that humans must be superior due to their intellect.

Even today some people think that animals are inferior to humans and are just another natural resource to be used for humankind's benefit. However, modern observations and research have left others no doubt that animals experience hap-

Animal Intelligence on Display

A 2014 article by Discovery Communications uses the achievements of animals like those listed below to illustrate the belief that humans are not the only intelligent species living on Earth:

- Crows' intelligence rivals that of seven-year-old humans with regard to cause and effect. One study reported that crows completed an "Aesop's fable paradigm" task in which they had to drop stones into water to make the water level rise, bringing food on top of the water closer to their reach.

- Honeybees show that larger brains do not necessarily mean higher intelligence: they can count, group similar objects like dogs or human faces, understand "same" and "different," and know the difference between shapes that are symmetrical and asymmetrical.

- Dogs can learn to understand between 165 and 250 words, and can also recognize and indicate errors in simple mathematical computations like $1 + 1 = 3$.

- Cockatoos, "animal master-burglars," can pick almost any lock. One adult male cockatoo named "Pipin" retrieved a nut after picking a lock that required him to remove a pin, screw, and bolt, then turn a wheel 90 degrees and shift a latch sideways—all in less than two hours.

- Fish can distinguish between larger and smaller quantities, "count" up to three, and know the difference between two pieces of classical music.

piness, sadness, fear, pain, anger, and boredom, just as humans do. They question whether people can continue to treat animals as they have done in the past, now that they know so much more about them.

Many people, however—perhaps influenced by animal-rights campaigners or their own experience of living or working with animals—recognize that animals may not be machines, but that they are still not quite human. They think it should be possible to use animals for the benefit of humanity without mistreating them, and that people should try to find ways of doing so.

Animal Intelligence and Feelings

Animals do not necessarily have to learn the same things that humans know in order to be called intelligent.

By the middle of the twentieth century, scientists were try-

Research has shown that primate behavior is similar in many ways to that of humans.

An Asian elephant male named Koshik can imitate human speech, speaking five words in Korean with a trunk instead of the lips that humans have. He is able to say, "annyong" ("hello"), "anja" ("sit down"), "aniya" ("no"), "nuo" ("lie down"), and "choah" ("good").

ing to find out how animals, including humans, learned things. Their results showed that many animal species altered their behavior in order to adapt to changing conditions. Rats, for example, could learn how to get to the middle of a maze to find food. This ability to change behavior according to circumstances made it clear that some animals are indeed intelligent.

Research has also shown that, just like humans, animals feel happy when things go their way and sad or angry when

In countries where farmers are too poor to afford tractors, or where wheeled vehicles cannot work, animals supply plow-pulling power.

they do not. If they are doing what they want, in the company of those they want to be with and in pleasant surroundings, they experience happiness. If they are deprived of their freedom or made to suffer in some way, they feel sadness, fear, pain, anger, and boredom.

Unhappy animals make their feelings plain. They whine, pace up and down, injure themselves, stop eating, or lash out at their neighbors. Swans, who mate for life, pine if their partner dies. A captive animal in a too-small cage will bang its head against the bars, pull its fur out, or simply sit and rock backwards and forwards.

Why Are Animals Hunted?

The view of the relationship between people and animals has historically been based on the idea that human interests are more important than those of animals. People hunt animals for food, clothing, and sport, and they use the land animals live on for their own purposes.

Most people in today's world no longer hunt animals in order to protect themselves or to survive, although some still

Some indigenous people, such as these San in Namibia, Africa, continue to hunt for their food using the traditional ways of their ancestors.

have to. Wild animals are now hunted for many reasons: for food, for their furs or skins, to keep their numbers down, and sometimes purely for enjoyment.

Why Hunt Animals for Food or Fur?

Some animals are now specially bred and farmed for humans to eat, but most still live in the wild. The meat of animals in the wild is highly prized because it is more difficult to get, and it can be sold for high prices. People in some parts of the world make a living from hunting or trapping animals that cannot be farmed and selling their meat or fur.

Some people hunt wild animals because they would not have meat to eat or clothes to wear if they did not. American Indians used the bison they hunted for many purposes to help their communities survive: meat for immediate food and dried jerky for later; horns for arrow points, eating utensils, and medication; fat for soap; bones for knives and shovels; bladders for food pouches and water containers; tendons for bowstrings; and hide for clothing. Today there remain some indigenous societies that still rely on hunting, including the San people of Africa's Kalahari Desert, aborigines in western Australia, native tribes in the Amazon rainforest of Brazil, and tribal groups living on isolated islands in the Pacific, such as Papua New Guinea and some of the Philippine and Indonesian islands.

Why Hunt Animals to Keep Numbers Down?

If too many animals share the same living space, both the animals and their environment can suffer. Animals have to com-

A herd of whitetail deer browses for food in the winter snow. In some of the populous states of the northeastern United States, such as New Jersey, Pennsylvania, and New York, growing deer herds have harmed forests and farms, and even affected humans when they have wandered into populated areas and onto highways. As a result, some communities have organized special hunts in order to control the wild deer populations, with mixed results.

pete with each other for food, and large numbers can mean there is not enough to go around.

Many wild animals are themselves food for others, and their numbers are controlled by predators. Some species have no natural predators and are *culled* by humans to keep numbers down.

People used to go on safari to kill wild animals for sport. They took home tusks, horns, antlers or skins as trophies. Now, they take photographs and videos as souvenirs.

Why Hunt Animals for Enjoyment?

People hunt animals for sport all over the world. They enjoy the challenge of tracking down and killing their prey. Sometimes they eat what they kill. It may be the size of what they catch or the number of animals caught that is important to hunters. In the United States (US), large mammals like deer and bears are targets. In the United Kingdom (UK), game birds like partridge, pheasant, and quail are all specially reared and hunted for sport. Game birds are not farmed in the same way that chickens are. They are protected while they breed, so they can be shot for food only at certain times of the year. In other European countries, wild birds like larks and blackbirds are hunted. Freshwater and sea-dwelling fish like salmon and tuna are hunted for sport and for food all over the world.

Some species of wild animals have been brought to the point of extinction by over-hunting or have had their habitats destroyed because of the way people use the land.

 # China's Bear Farms

While attitudes on the treatment of wild animals are changing in many countries, in others they remain the same, as this report on bear farms in China indicates. "In a tiny iron cage, too small to allow him to stand up or lie down, a young Asiatic black bear is huddled in agony. His stomach is permanently oozing thick, yellow bile from an open wound. Twice a day, a metal tube will be forcibly inserted through the wound into his gallbladder, and he will be systematically 'milked' of his bile, which will be used in traditional Chinese medicine, cosmetics, and even wine. . . . In hundreds of bear farms across China, thousands of bears are kept in such conditions. Often taken from the wild, the best they can hope for is a swift death from the pain and shock of the initial operation to open their gall bladder. If they are unfortunate enough to survive, then they are condemned to between five and ten years of torment before their bile dries up and they are simply abandoned. . . ."

The intelligence of many creatures can be seen in their everyday behavior. Some have figured out how to use tools to make their lives easier, such as this ruddy turnstone, which smashes a mussel's shell against a stone to get at its next meal.

Why Are Animals Farmed?

Although some wild creatures—tuna, whales, and seals, for example—are still hunted for food, other animals have been farmed as humans realized it was easier to keep them nearby and under control. Cattle, sheep, and goats have been domesticated so that their meat, milk, and skins would be readily available. While animals like sheep, kept for their valuable wool, do not necessarily have to die for human use, other animals must die for humans to make use of their resources.

Some people who recognize that there are good reasons why animals are farmed for food find it hard to accept that they should be kept and killed for other purposes.

Are Animals Farmed Just for Food?

Some wild animals, such as mink, are kept confined on fur farms so that their skins can be made into clothes and other luxury goods. In the wild, mink have large territories and roam freely. However, when kept captive in cages, they show many signs of stress. They are killed when they are about seven months old, when their winter coat is fully developed. The killing methods—lethal injection, electrocution, or gassing—are chosen so as not to damage their valuable skins.

The United States Department of Agriculture (USDA) reported in 2010 that there were 265 mink farms that produced 2.82 million pelts valued at $231 million ($81.90 per pelt). Such farms are also widespread in the UK, Holland, Scandinavia, Russia, and Canada. Besides mink, these farms raise and kill foxes, raccoons, and wild cats for their fur.

 # Text-Dependent Questions

1. What did Charles Darwin mean by the phrase "survival of the fittest"?
2. Name three reasons humans hunt animals.
3. Why are animals farmed? Give examples of specific animals.

 # Research Project

Some believe animals think, feel, and suffer just like humans. Maybe they cannot speak or write like people do, but they can still experience the same kinds of emotions. Others argue that animals' responses are not the same as the complex emotions humans feel. Giving them names and treating them like humans is inappropriate. Using the Internet or your school library, do some research on animal feelings, and answer the following question: "Are animals sentient (feeling) beings?" Write a two-page report, using data you have found in your research to support your conclusion, and present it to your class.

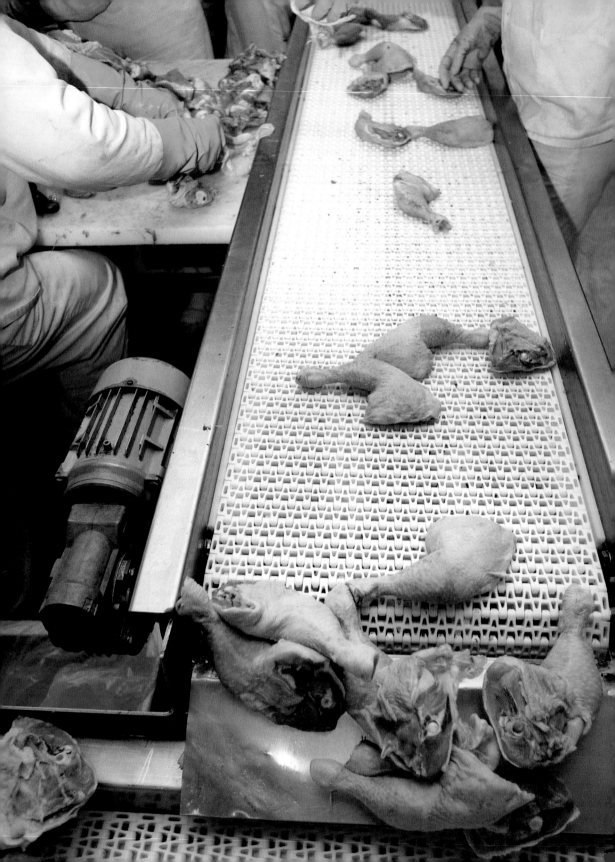

Animals Raised for Food

Most people in the Western world buy their food. They rely on farmers for food because they no longer have the desire, space, time, or knowledge to raise animals for meat, eggs, and dairy products. Price is an important issue; people have learned to expect cheap food.

In the United States, more than 8.54 billion chickens are slaughtered every year. The annual total for fish is 6 billion; for pigs, 100 million; and for cattle the figure is 42 million. Generally speaking, animals bred for food are no longer slaughtered by the farmers who raised them. Some are transported hundreds of miles to *abattoirs* to be killed.

Just as carmakers in the early twentieth century realized that they could manufacture and sell their goods cheaply if they produced enough of them and sold them at the right price, so

Millions of chickens are slaughtered, plucked and gutted every day in poultry-processing factories. Industrial systems are necessary to provide enough fresh food and meat for people, but animal rights activists often complain about the cruelty of slaughterhouses as well as of industrial farming operations.

did farmers. Factory farming began in the 1920s when scientists discovered that if certain vitamins were added to animal feed, the animals did not need sunlight and exercise in order to grow. Farmers could rear large numbers of animals indoors year-round and combat any resulting diseases with newly discovered antibiotic medicines. The American Society for the Prevention of Cruelty to Animals (ASPCA) defines factory farms as intensive industrial operations that raise mass numbers of animals for food, and they account for 99 percent of farm animals in the United States. ASPCA details conditions for different animals on intensive farms below.

Chicken Farming

Chickens which are kept outdoors naturally scratch at the ground, perch, dust-bathe, and make nests. However, nearly 90 percent of laying hens—300 million in the U.S. alone—are reared indoors in "battery" cages that are smaller than an 8.5-

 Words to Understand in This Chapter

abattoir—slaughterhouse.

loophole—an error in the way a law, rule, or contract is written that makes it possible for some people to legally avoid obeying it.

media—means of mass communication such as the Internet, newspapers, magazines, television, and radio.

retailer—business that sells directly to customers; where most people get their food.

udder—the bag-shaped part of their body where milk is produced and stored.

by-11-inch sheet of paper. In the U.S. over 8.54 billion chickens are killed for their meat each year. They are specially bred so they grow quickly, but being overweight in crowded conditions

More than 300 million hens are used by the U.S. egg industry every year. Many hens are kept on commercial egg farms, where they are packed into cages and fed antibiotic-rich food. Their environment is stimulated to maximize their egg laying, and conditions are often unsanitary. Hens usually only live about two years on these farms.

Factory-farmed chickens raised for their meat are kept indoors, thousands to each shed, and are fed a special diet so that they put on weight quickly.

can lead to bone deformities and lameness before they are slaughtered at six weeks old.

All birds are excluded from federal animal protection laws, and by sheer numbers, birds are the most abused type of animal in the United States. There are two types of chickens on intensive farms: egg-laying hens and chickens raised for meat. Only female chickens can lay eggs and have the body type to be used for meat. With no market demand for male chicks, they are usually killed by grinding, gassing, crushing, or suffocation.

Egg-laying hens are kept in individual battery cages, or up to

10 may be packed together in a cage the size of a file drawer. When a hen's egg production slows down, some farms deny the hen proper nutrition for two weeks, shocking the hen's body into one final laying cycle before it is killed and used as meat.

Chickens raised for meat are crammed in large sheds where they live on top of their own waste. A combination of antibiotics, over-feeding, and lack of exercise lead to chickens with large breasts and weaker skeletons and organs. Many have difficulty breathing and supporting their own weight, and exist in chronic pain. While chickens can naturally live for up to 10

Free-range poultry are allowed to scratch and peck outside. They take longer to grow to full size, and their meat and eggs cost more to buy.

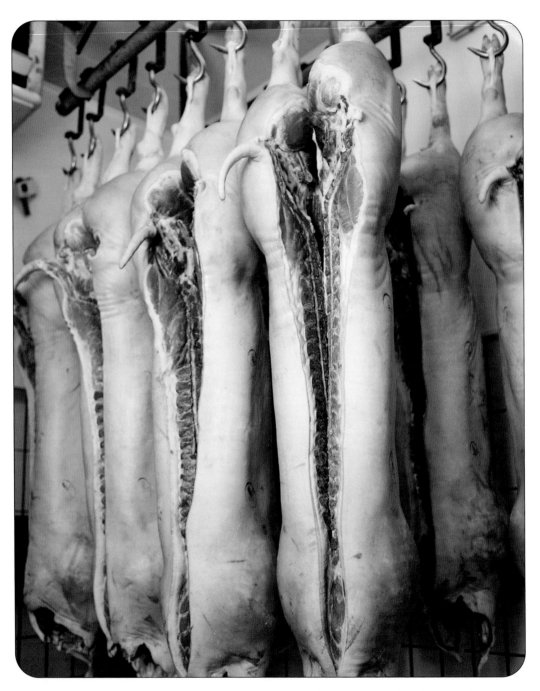

The carcasses of freshly slaughtered pigs hang in the freezer room of a slaughterhouse.

years, most on factory farms are killed when they are six weeks old.

Pork Farming

In the United States, virtually all of the 100 million pigs raised for food are from intensive factory farms. Both male and female pigs are used for food, and though they can live up to 15 years, most are killed at six months old.

On factory farms, pregnant sows typically give birth in a special crate in which they are unable to make a nest for their piglets or even turn around. Male baby pigs are often castrated because consumers do not like the smell or taste of uncastrated male pigs.

At two to three weeks old, these young pigs are taken from their mothers and packed in windowless sheds where they stand in their own waste and cannot move adequately. Research has shown that pigs are intelligent animals—at least as smart as dogs. They are curious and need mental stimulation. However, in these crowded sheds they are not able to explore. Frustrated pigs may bite others' tails, so farmers often cut off tails beforehand—without using painkillers.

Cattle Farming

Many intensively farmed, milk-producing cattle spend much of their time indoors. In order to produce milk, they must have given birth to a calf. Their calves are taken away soon after birth, and the mothers are milked by machines. Dairy cattle are bred specially for their milk-producing ability and may have *udders* so big that they find it difficult to walk. They are given

People and Meat

According to a 2011 study by the Worldwatch Institute, Pork is the most widely consumed meat in the world, followed by poultry, beef, and mutton. Here are some other interesting facts from that study:

- People in the developing world eat 71 pounds of meat per year on average, compared to 176 pounds per person in the industrial world.
- Of the 880 million rural poor people living on less than $1 per day, 70 percent are partially or completely dependent on livestock for food and to make a living.
- Raising farm animals accounts for roughly 23 percent of all global water use in farming.
- Eighty percent of all antibiotics are used on farm animals, compared to 20 percent used for human illnesses.
- Eating organic, pasture-raised animals can be healthier and more environmentally beneficial compared to intensive farming systems.

hormones to raise their level of milk production to 100 pounds per day. The unnaturally high milk production often leads to a bacterial infection called mastitis, which causes painful swelling in the udders. To keep milk flowing, cows are artificially impregnated each year, leaving them pregnant for most of their lives.

Beef cattle breeds are selected for their ability to gain weight quickly and efficiently, and they may be given special hormones to make them grow even more rapidly. Though cattle can naturally live up to 25 years, beef cattle are often killed at one to three years of age. They often begin their lives grazing on open pasture, but the last months of life are usually

Intensively farmed milk-producing cattle are specially bred, separated from their calves, fed on concentrates and milked by machines.

spent crowded on barren feedlots that provide little shelter and no room to avoid standing in their own waste. Here, beef cows can suffer from digestive disorders due to the unnatural food they are forced to eat. Many are branded, castrated, and de-horned without the use of painkillers.

Male offspring are raised for veal while females become the next generation of dairy cows. In some European countries where veal is a delicacy, milk-fed calves are kept in small crates and slaughtered when they are very young.

Fish Farming

Farmed fish are raised in cages or pens suspended in lakes, bays, or coastal waters before they are killed for sale. Shellfish, such as oysters and mussels, are also farmed.

People for the Ethical Treatment of Animals (PETA) reports more than 40 percent of all fish consumed each year are from land- or ocean-based aquafarms where fish spend their lives in cramped, enclosed waters. Fish on these farms may suffer from parasitic infections, diseases, and injuries, with up to 40 percent being blind on some farms. Crowding causes sores and damage to fins. Profits increase if more fish are housed in smaller areas, so some salmon may spend their entire lives in a space the size of a bathtub, while 27 trout may live in the same-sized space.

Farmed fish are given powerful antibiotics to help them survive diseases and filthy water from their waste. It is likely that living in their own waste is the cause of toxins found in farmed fish at levels seven times higher than fish in the wild.

Fish are often starved, for as long as 10 days, before being

Wild salmon travel many miles between their breeding grounds and open water, often leaping spectacularly as they travel upstream to mate. Farmed salmon are kept in large pens.

sent to slaughter in order to reduce waste contamination of the water during transport. In the U.S., fish are not stunned, so they are conscious when they start down the slaughter line. Their gills are cut, and they are left to bleed to death. Other fish, including salmon, are sometimes hit on the head before being cut open. Smaller fish, such as trout, are often killed by simply draining away their water environment and letting them die of suffocation.

How Does Intensive Farming Affect Animals?

Farmers have learned how to regulate animals' breeding cycles so that eggs are laid or new animals are born at convenient times.

Animals living under natural conditions—where the number of daylight hours, for example, varies with the time of year—eat, sleep, and breed at certain times, depending on the daylight. Animals kept indoors are exposed to artificial daylight for longer hours to produce eggs or young more often than they would naturally.

Many intensively farmed animals live in enclosures designed for easy cleaning and waste disposal rather than for their comfort. Many can barely move and have no access to the outdoors. Animals kept in confined spaces may turn on each other or on themselves because they are kept in unnaturally tight spaces that cause them mental and physical distress.

Poultry may have their beaks trimmed, so they cannot cause damage by pecking. Horned cattle routinely have their horns removed. Some chickens actually become deformed because they do not have enough space to grow properly, and others may be crushed or trampled to death.

Diseases and parasites spread quickly through animal communities kept in enclosed spaces. They may have to be treated with powerful antibiotics that can remain in their meat after they are killed.

For many pigs that are raised on commercial farms, the only time they will breathe fresh air is when they are loaded onto the truck that will take them to the slaughterhouse.

The ASPCA reports standard intensive farming practices create a host of unhealthy conditions for the many animals that are raised:

- Unclean air: Waste piles up in the animal sheds, creating ammonia and dust. The ammonia irritates, and can even burn, animals' eyes, skin, and throats.
- Unnatural growth: Fast and disproportionate growth and production due to selective breeding causes ailments including chronic pain, mobility problems, and heart problems.
- Unnatural reproduction: Many female farm animals spend virtually their entire lives pregnant, putting them under chronic strain.
- Absent veterinary care: Most factory farms deny animals individualized veterinary care, including humane euthanasia.
- Surgical mutilations: Many farm animals undergo painful mutilations to their tails, testicles, horns, toes, or beaks, without painkillers, to make their behavior more manageable.
- Shortened lives: Factory farmed animals are generally slaughtered at "market weight," well before the end of their natural life spans. In fact, most are still babies.

Slaughterhouse Practices

Most sheep and pigs are stunned by having an electric current passed through their brains. Cattle and some sheep are stunned by having a bolt fired from a special pistol into their brains at very high speed. Their throats are then cut so that they bleed to death.

Poultry slaughter is highly mechanized. The birds are hung upside down by their legs from shackles attached to a moving line, similar to a conveyor belt. The line drags the birds' heads through a stunning bath filled with electrified water. Once stunned, or sometimes killed, the moving line then takes them to automatic neck-cutters. Turkeys are killed in a similar way, except that their necks are cut by hand.

 # The Rules of Religious Slaughter

Many Hindus are vegetarians because they believe that harming any living thing is wrong.

Muslims may only eat *halal* meat, which must come from animals slaughtered in a particular way. There are religious rules for this, including special prayers that must be said during the slaughter of an animal. Under *halal* restrictions, during the slaughtering process the animal must be conscious while the blood is drained from its bodies.

Jews must eat only kosher meat, which comes from animals slaughtered according to Jewish rules by a qualified butcher. The slaughtered animal's blood must be allowed to drain from its body through a slit in its throat.

Sikhs who eat meat will do so only if it is *Jhatka*, which means it comes from an animal that has been killed with a single stroke. They cannot eat *halal* meat.

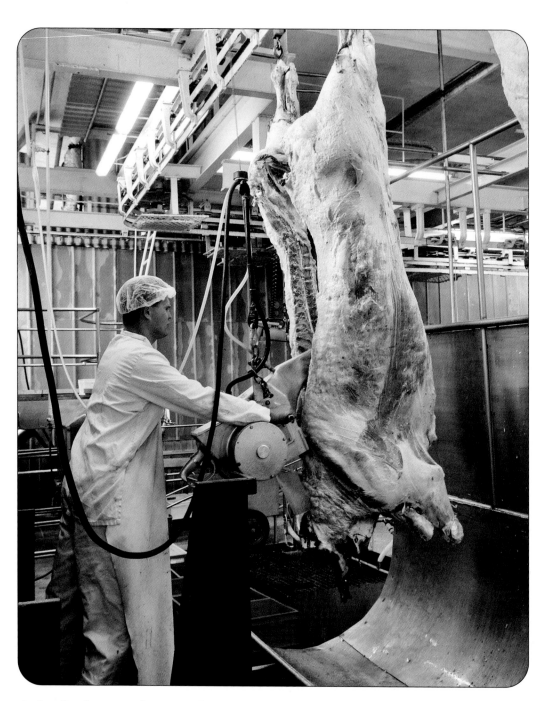

A slaughterhouse worker uses a large saw to cut a cow's carcass in half.

Research has shown that animals can be stressed when they are unloaded from the vehicles taking them for slaughter due to rough handling and unfamiliar noises and smells that surround them. If they are not properly stunned, they may be conscious and feel pain when they are actually killed.

State and Federal Laws that Protect Farm Animals

The ASPCA states that the U.S. has no federal laws protecting animals actually living on farms, but two federal laws cover farm animals during transport and slaughter. All poultry are excluded from these protections.

The 28-Hour Law requires that animals transported on land across state lines for slaughter be unloaded every 28 hours for rest, food, and water. However, this law has many *loopholes* that allow people to avoid obeying it.

The Humane Methods of Livestock Slaughter Act (HMLSA) requires that livestock be stunned, unable to feel pain, before being slaughtered. Poultry are not protected by this act, and it also exempts certain forms of religious slaughter, such as Kosher and Halal.

The majority of American states do not include farm animals in their anti-cruelty provisions, making it nearly impossible to provide even basic protections. Some states that include farm animals in at least some of their anti-cruelty laws rarely enforce them.

However, an increasing number of states are banning particular practices such as cruel methods of confinement and tail cutting of cows.

Advantages of Intensive Farming

The world's human population is growing rapidly and needs to be fed. Farms are becoming bigger and more efficient. Machinery is replacing human and animal labor. New drugs mean that diseases that might once have wiped out large numbers of livestock can be controlled. Farmers can buy new kinds of animal feed based on concentrated nutrients and supplement their animals' diets with hormones to make them grow faster.

All over the world, intensive farming is now supplying affordable meat. In countries where there are more people than

People all over the world, like these Haitian schoolchildren, are sick or dying because they cannot get enough to eat.

Even in a wealthy country, such as the United States, about 48 million people are do not have access to adequate, nutritious food.

the land can easily support using traditional farming methods, intensive farming may offer a way of reducing malnutrition and starvation. It might not mean happy animals, but it does result in the production of cheap and plentiful food for humans.

With intensive farming, animals can be selected and bred for their ability to produce low-cost, high-quality food for humans. Meat and dairy products are now available year-round rather than only at certain times.

Intensive farming methods mean that the same amount of

land can be made to produce more food and a greater variety of it. People have more choices about what to buy and eat.

Because supermarkets buy huge quantities of meat and dairy products, they can demand that farmers produce high-quality foodstuffs that are then sold at a relatively low cost.

Research shows that for many people, price is the most important factor when it comes to choosing food. Foodstuffs produced by intensive farming methods are cheaper than those that are not.

The Human Cost of Intensive Farming

The trend of fewer and larger farms, coupled with the use of machines rather than human labor, means fewer agricultural jobs. Many "traditional" farmers, unable to compete with their giant neighbors for a share of the market, have gone out of business or are in serious financial trouble.

Food safety has also become a big issue. It has been shown that some life-threatening animal diseases may be passed on to humans who eat tainted meat, and some people think that modern farming methods are partly to blame. Farms that are not properly maintained can be breeding grounds for danger- ous bacteria like salmonella and E. coli, which can be passed to humans through meat, dairy, and eggs.

To prevent people from getting sick, intensive farms feed animals large doses of antibiotics. However, overuse of antibi- otics can lead to the development of drug-resistant strains of bacteria, which can spread to human consumers. In addition, 75 percent of the antibiotics used on livestock are not absorbed

The expansion of industrial farming techniques has made it harder for small family farmers to make a good living.

by the animals and are excreted in waste, posing a serious risk to public health.

Human environments also suffer negative consequences from intensive farming. Animal waste from intensive farms pollutes the water, land, and air in neighboring communities. Livestock account for an estimated 18 percent of human-caused greenhouse gas emissions, producing 40 percent of the world's methane and 65 percent of the world's nitrous oxide.

Farms consume massive quantities of precious limited resources, including water and fossil fuels. Plant-eating fish may be fed fish oil and fish meal to make them bigger, and carnivorous fish are fed smaller fish from already depleted oceans. Feeding fish on farms can exhaust the population in the wild, as it can take more than five pounds of ocean fish to produce one pound of farmed salmon or sea bass.

What Is the Alternative?

More and more people are becoming unhappy about the way their food is produced. They worry that the drugs and hormones fed to animals will end up in their own bodies when they eat meat, eggs, or dairy products.

Animal-welfare organizations all over the world have drawn attention to the way livestock is treated on intensive farms. They say that animals are being treated like machines and kept in unnatural, unhealthy conditions that cause them severe distress. Others point out that most people in the USA are not starving, and farmers are supplying far more food than is actually needed.

Supermarkets and other *retailers* have enormous influence on what farmers produce. They can refuse to accept meat that has too much fat on it or is the wrong color or shape. What they buy from farmers depends on what their customers say they want and how much they are prepared to pay.

Many supermarkets and other food suppliers are now offering people a choice. They can either buy cheap, mass-produced food or pay more for something else. Eggs from chickens confined in battery cages cost less than eggs produced by chickens kept indoors on straw. These, in turn, are cheaper than free-range eggs laid by hens that can run about outside.

Animals are said to be farmed organically if they are raised on land that has not been treated by pesticides, fed a "natural" diet that does not include antibiotics or growth-promoters, given room to roam freely, and slaughtered in a way that does not cause them pain. Rearing animals this way costs more, but it is thought to be kinder to them. Sales of organically farmed produce are rising in developed countries.

Governments want to make sure that their citizens have enough to eat. They offer farmers money to produce more of certain foods, or pay them to use their land in specific ways. The *media* influence what happens by reporting on current events. They also give publicity to groups and individuals trying to change the way people think.

 ## Text-Dependent Questions

1. What is the definition of a factory farm?
2. Name five unhealthy conditions for animals on intensive factory farms.
3. What are the rules for slaughtering animals in Islam and Judaism?
4. How does intensive farming affect human environments?
5. What are the characteristics of organically-farmed animals?

 ## Research Project

Using the Internet or your school library, do some research on farmed animals, and answer the following question: "Does it matter how farmed animals are kept?" Some think people would not mind paying a bit more for food if it meant animals were better treated. Others say farmers have a duty to provide food at low prices so that it's available to everyone, and it does not matter how they do it. Write a two-page report, using data you have found in your research to support your conclusion, and present it to your class.

Animals and Entertainment

Humans all over the world are entertained by animals. They visit zoos and circuses where animals are on display and attend sporting events where animals are the star performers. Popular films and television programs feature both wild and domesticated animals, and many people keep animals as pets.

For many years, the only chance most people got to see wild animals was when they went to the zoo. Those were the days before television and film brought animals into people's homes almost on a daily basis.

Zoo visitors used to find examples of mammals, birds, amphibians, and reptiles kept in cages of varying sizes and almost close enough to touch. Protests about the conditions under which the animals were kept became common in the sec-

Thoroughbred horse racing is a multi-billion dollar entertainment industry that is popular in the United States, Canada, the United Kingdom, in many countries of the European Union, and throughout South America.

ond half of the twentieth century. Things began to change as people realized how far the cages were from the animals' natural habitats.

Today's zoos, including safari and farm parks, are much more likely to keep their animals uncaged and out in the open. Some run *conservation* programs and breeding projects to help build up the numbers of endangered species. Certain animals, like the giant panda, however, are famous for their determination not to let humans interfere with their sex lives and will not breed to order.

How Are Circus Animals Treated?

Circus visits are a popular form of entertainment in many parts of the world. Besides clowns, jugglers, fire-eaters, and acrobats, people can see elephants, primates, dogs, horses, and lions obeying the commands of their trainers and performing all kinds of tricks.

In many countries, animal-welfare campaigners have drawn attention to the way circus and other performing animals are treated. They point out that they are often kept in cramped conditions and made to learn behavior that is confus-

 Words to Understand in This Chapter

conservation—a careful preservation and protection of animals, plants, and natural resources.

negligent—failing to take proper or normal care of something or someone.

Many exotic creatures, such as these parrots, are flown thousands of miles from their natural habitats to become household pets. Not all survive the journey.

ing and not natural for them.

Sometimes circus-animal training involves punishment for getting things wrong. Trainers use whips, tight collars, muzzles, electric prods, bullhooks, and other painful tools to get animals to obey orders. Some high-profile court cases in the later years of the twentieth century saw circus owners convicted of cruelty, and many of today's traveling circuses feature few, if any, animals. In the US, no government agency monitors training sessions, though more and more communities are banning or restricting the use of animals in circuses.

Performing animals such as bears, for example, are still highly prized in some parts of the world, and they provide a valuable source of income for their owners.

How Are Animals Involved in Sport?

Horse racing is now a worldwide industry worth billions of dollars. Fortunes are made and lost by not only the bettors of horse races, but also the owners, breeders, and trainers of some of the most valuable animals in the world. These horses have

Greyhound dogs that run in races are often drugged to hide sickness and injury. Between races, they are often confined to cramped stalls or crates for most of each day. After a few years, when dogs are no longer able to race, many of them are euthanized, sold to laboratories for experiments, or sent to slaughterhouses.

Well-bred animals may be trained to compete in special events intended to showcase the most desirable features of their breed, such as the annual Westminster Kennel Club Dog Show.

their mates carefully chosen for them by humans, so their offspring will, they hope, win some of the huge cash prizes offered in competitions and go on to produce future winners themselves. Even people who do not deal with the actual horses, such as those working in betting shops, make money from the sport.

Other animals raced for human sport include dogs and camels. Specially bred pigeons are released miles away from where they live to see which can get home fastest.

Bullfighting

Bullfighting is a popular form of entertainment in Spain, Portugal, Mexico, and other Latin American countries. A bullfight begins when the bull comes into a specially built arena to be greeted by the matador for a fight that lasts around 15 minutes. A fighting bull charges instantly at anything that moves because of its natural instinct and centuries of special breeding. The matador must kill it or be killed.

Picadors first weaken the bull by stabbing it from horseback. Banderillos then approach the bull on foot to attack its shoulders with barbed sticks and make it lower its head so the matador can kill it.

The matador uses his cape to attract the bull's attention, getting closer and closer to its horns in order to excite the crowd. By now the bull is aware that its life is in danger and, though weakened by the picadors and banderillos, is still dangerous and could kill the matador with one swipe of his horns.

The matador eventually kills the bull by stabbing it between the shoulder blades, sometimes leaping over its horns as hc docs so.

In recent years some countries have made bullfighting illegal, as it is considered animal cruelty. In the region of Catalonia, Spain, it was outlawed in 2012. Bullfighting has also been banned in three Mexican states: Sonora in 2013, Guerrero in 2014 and Coahuila in 2015.

Some sports, like cockfighting and dogfighting, have been outlawed because the aim is for one animal to kill its opponent. If people are caught participating in these sports, they can be imprisoned. Others sports that often result in the likely death of an animal, are legal in the countries where these practices originated or are an important part of the culture, such as bull-fighting in Spain and Latin America. However, these sports are generally disapproved of elsewhere.

In 2007, NFL quarterback Michael Vick was sentenced to

Cockfighting, which pits two trained roosters in a fight held in a ring, is illegal in the United States. However, in other countries, the sport is very popular. The participating birds are often badly injured or killed during the event, but spectators, such as these people in Thailand, bet their money on the outcome and enjoy the spectacle.

In the United States, there are nearly 75 million pet cats, more than 69 million pet dogs, over 8.3 million pet birds, and roughly 4.9 million pet horses.

23 months in prison for his involvement in a dogfighting operation in which pit bulls were tortured and killed. After being released from prison, Vick became a spokesperson for the Humane Society of the United States, and has spoken publicly about proper care for animals and the end of dogfighting.

Animal-welfare pressure groups continue to raise awareness of cruel practices both at home and abroad in the hope that they can be stopped. Many people nowadays get their pets from animal-rescue centers instead of breeders or importers.

What about Pet Animals?

Many people want animals as pets or companions, and there are breeders and importers who make money by supplying this demand. Some animals are taken from the wild, while others are specially bred. Although many dogs and cats have comfortable homes, nutritious food, and loving guardians, others suffer at the hands of *negligent* or abusive owners, live on city streets, or are kept in animal shelters that may put them down if they are not adopted within a certain time period.

Many people have pets, and most are of the cute, furry variety—cats, dogs, rabbits, hamsters, and guinea pigs—but snakes, spiders, birds, and fish also share some humans' homes. Some people think that children who have pets grow up better able to take responsibility for creatures other than themselves, while others keep them simply for the pleasure and company they provide. Some researchers claim that stroking a cat or dog can help a person lower their stress levels; others say that people living alone have longer, healthier lives if they share their home with a pet.

The animal rights organization People Against Commercial Kennels (PACK) march in New York against puppy mills and pet stores that sell the offspring.

Many animals sold in pet shops have been specially bred for sale and are products just like chocolate or breakfast cereal. Sometimes they are kept in cramped conditions and not looked after properly. The people who buy them are not checked out to make sure they can offer a proper home, and organizations such as the Humane Society may be called to rescue pets that have been abandoned or mistreated—like Salt and Pepper. Salt and Pepper, two adult male cats, were taken to a rescue center after being abandoned in a dumped car. They were in a cardboard box barely big enough for one cat and had spent about five days without food or water. They were petrified of people and tried to attack anyone who came near them. Careful training and lots of patience by the rescue center staff led to them eventually finding new homes.

 ## Text-Dependent Questions

1. What animal sports have been outlawed and why?
2. What are three benefits companion animals can provide to people?

 ## Research Project

Using the Internet or your school library, do some research on animals in sport, and answer the following question: "Should animals be used in sport?" Some contend that sport animals are well-cared for and that sports promote human-animal relationships. Others argue that animals are forced into training to perform unnatural tasks, and that they are being exploited for human amusement. Write a two-page report, using data you have found in your research to support your conclusion, and present it to your class.

5

Animals and Medical Research

The brain structures of humans and chimpanzees are nearly the same. Many scientific studies have identified specific similarities, noting that humans and chimpanzees have a DNA match of 98.8 percent. Humans now understand a lot about their own behavior as a result of tests done on animals and regularly use drugs and other products that animal tests have shown to be safe.

Humans have shared their world with other animals for millions of years, but it is only in the last few centuries that they have truly realized how much can be learned from them.

Early explorers, who left their own countries in search of valuable goods or wanted simply to find out what was "out there," brought back tales of extraordinary creatures their fellow citizens had never seen and could hardly believe. The first

Chagas Disease is a form of sleeping sickness found only in the Americas, and specially bred rodents are used to research its cause and possible cure.

rhinoceros brought to London had people running for cover because they had never been exposed to such an animal.

The idea that these species were anything other than curiosities did not surface for a long time. When scientists suggested animals might actually have a lot in common with humans, people were aghast.

What Can We Learn from Animals?

It is now known that humans are not the only animals to live in social groups and build complex, organized societies. Humans may not be able to understand other species' languages, but research has shown that many animals do communicate with their own kind—warn them of danger, express affection, and show each other where the food is.

Some animals are very much like humans. When Darwin suggested in the late nineteenth century that humankind descended from apes, there was uproar. Most people now agree that his ideas make sense, but some still object to them. Researchers continue to study animals to find out how they and their communities work—sometimes in search of knowledge for its own sake, sometimes to see if there are any lessons

 Words to Understand in This Chapter

therapeutic—of or relating to the treatment of illnesses by methods that produce positive, healing effects.

xenotransplant—transplantation of an organ, tissue, or cells between two different species, especially from an animal to a human.

The genetic relationship between humans and chimpanzees is so close, some modern scientists have noted that homo sapiens could properly be classified as a third species of chimpanzee.

humans can learn from them.

Some animals' brains and bodies are so like humans' that scientists believe what works for them will work for people too. If an animal's body reacts badly to something it comes into contact with, the chances are that a person's will as well. If an animal remains fit and healthy with a product or medicine, the likelihood is that humans will as well. Animals have been used to test whether products like shampoo, eye make-up, laundry detergent, shower gel, and toothpaste are safe for humans to use.

Drugs used by vets to prevent and treat animal illnesses are tested on other animals first, to make sure they are safe.

Scientists now know that pigs' bodies are very similar to humans'. Medical researchers have discovered that organs transplanted into humans from pigs are less likely to be rejected than those from other animals. Specially-treated pigskin makes a superb temporary bandage on human burns because it prevents infection and allows the patient's damaged skin to repair itself. Scientists have not yet worked out a way of getting hold of a pig's heart, kidney, or skin that does not negatively affect the pig.

Organ Transplants from Animals

Xenotransplantation is the term for a procedure in which live cells, tissues, or organs are transplanted from a nonhuman animal source into a human. The idea of xenotransplantation is, in part, driven by the fact that the demand for human organs for clinical transplantation far exceeds the supply. Currently, ten patients die each day in the United States while on the waiting list to receive lifesaving vital organ transplants, according to the US Food and Drug Administration (FDA).

According to the FDA, baboons and pigs are the best xenotransplant donors. Baboons are genetically close to humans, but carry some dangerous viruses. Also, they are in shorter supply than pigs.

A pig's body is strikingly similar to a human's. Pigs are generally healthier than primates and extremely easy to breed, producing a whole litter of piglets at a time rather than a single offspring as a baboon does. Additionally, there are fewer objections to killing pigs on moral grounds, since they are already slaughtered for food.

Despite the potential benefits, xenotransplantation raises concerns regarding the potential infection of human recipients with animal retroviruses that are not currently a problem among humans.

Does Research Harm the Animals It Uses?

If observed sensitively, animals in the wild hardly notice researchers are there. The researchers want to see what animals do naturally, not to interfere and change things.

Other research methods are different. New products like cosmetics and shampoos are often tested on animals to see if they are safe. They may be dropped into animals' eyes or rubbed into their skin. The number of animals that are used in this kind of research is now falling.

Scientists who want to find out what happens when new medicines are given to human patients are required by law to test them on animals first. Some current, powerful anti-cancer drugs that cause unpleasant side effects in human patients were tested on animals before they were ever given to people.

In 1959, British scientists W.M.S. Russell and R.I. Burch published *The Principles of Humane Experimental Techniques*. They suggested that researchers should follow the "Three 'R's": refine tests to minimize animal pain or distress, reduce the numbers of animals used, and try to replace animals by other methods of testing whenever they could. The number of animals used in product testing has fallen steadily since the 1970s.

Why Clone Animals?

New animal parts—or, in a few cases, a complete animal—can now be made by means of a process called cloning. In a 2015 article, CNN documented facts about animal cloning, explaining that reproductive cloning results in a full copy of an organ-

Dolly the sheep was the world's first animal to be cloned from an adult sheep cell, rather than from a fertilized egg. Dolly was cloned in 1996 and lived for almost seven years, before dying in February 2003 from a lung disease. This is fairly young by the usual standards, as sheep typically live to be 11 or 12 years old. However, scientists determined that her death was not a result of the cloning process. Since then, other animals have also been successfully cloned.

Humans have an important role to play in protecting wild species, such as sea turtles. Rescue centers care for wild or domesticated animals that are sick, neglected or abused. They either release animals back into the wild or try to find them good homes.

ism, while *therapeutic* cloning involves copying a specific part of the body for transplant. Dolly the sheep was reproductively cloned from an adult sheep in 1996, and since then, animals like pigs, goats, dogs, and horses have been cloned.

Some people believe that cloning will lead to great medical advances for humans. If a human's heart does not work properly, perhaps a spare one could be cloned for them out of one of their own cells or created using another animal's tissue for transplantation into them.

Maybe animal organs, such as livers or kidneys, could be injected with human genes, so that the body of a person receiving one of them in a transplant would not reject it. *Xenotransplants* could one day be a way of treating patients who now have to wait until a suitable human organ becomes available. The Mayo Clinic states that 90,000 people in the US are on the waiting list for a transplant, but only 25,000 organs are available annually.

What Are the Alternatives to Using Animals?

Over the last fifty years or so, growing numbers of people have decided that humans should not treat animals as they used to. There are ways of living and working that either avoid using animals for the benefit of humans or use them with greater respect.

Vegetarians choose not to eat meat and get the protein they need from plant-based sources. Vegans do not eat or use any animal products: they do not eat meat, milk, or eggs and do not wear leather or wool.

Animals in Laboratory Experiments

Worldwide, millions of animals are experimented on every year to test the possible effects of drugs and other new products, such as cosmetics and household chemicals, on humans and the environment. Here are some facts about animals used for laboratory research:

- In the United States and and European countries, about 29 million animals per year are used in research. Rats and mice make up around 80 percent of this total.
- The number of animals used in laboratory experiments in the United States and European Union has been reduced by half since the 1970s.
- In Canada, mammals have largely been replaced by fish in experiments.
- In the US and the EU, a drug's efficacy and safety must be tested in animals before it enters human testing. In 2010, the EU commission ruled that alternatives to animal testing must be used when possible.

Sources: USDA Animal and Plant Health Inspection Service; BBC.com.

Some vegetarians and vegans choose this lifestyle because they do not want to support current food-production methods, or they are concerned that animal diseases and the drugs given to cure them may remain in meat and harmful to the humans who eat it. Others live this way because they do not believe that humans have the right to eat their fellow creatures.

Leather and fur can now be replaced by man-made substitutes, and animal products once used in the manufacture of household goods, such as soap and cosmetics, have been replaced by chemical substitutes that do not involve animals at all.

Modern industrialized countries rarely use working animals to provide the power to drive machines. Power comes from other sources such as gas, oil, electricity, water, and wind. Any working animals that remain in use are protected from mistreatment by law.

 # Text-Dependent Questions

1. How are animals used in research?
2. What is the difference between reproductive cloning and therapeutic cloning?
3. What are alternatives to using animals for food, clothing, entertainment, and animal-tested drugs?

 # Research Project

Using the Internet or your school library, do some research on xenotransplants, and answer the following question: "Should animal organs be transplanted into humans?" Some believe xenotransplants are useful because animal organs are more plentiful and can be genetically altered, so the patient's body does not reject them. Thousands of human lives could be saved every year. Others maintain that animals carry many known viruses, and possibly some that have not been discovered yet. They could be introduced to the human population by xenotransplants, and prove deadly. Write a two-page report, using data you have found in your research to support your conclusion, and present it to your class.

6

Animal Rights Today

The animal-rights movement is made up of many groups of people scattered throughout the world. They do not all believe in exactly the same things or use the same tactics to influence people, but they all use newspapers, television, radio, and the Internet to publicize their beliefs and get laws changed.

Animal-rights campaigners use the media because it is an effective way of getting their ideas across to large numbers of people. They hope that if enough people agree with them, politicians will be forced to make laws that safeguard animals' rights and punish those who break them.

Does the Law Protect Animals?

Although there are laws in many countries that define how humans can treat animals, animals still do not have legal rights

An animal trainer performs with an orca, or killer whale, at the Sea World park in Florida. In recent years Sea World has been criticized by animal rights activists for its treatment of captive orcas. In 2015, the company announced that it would expand the living spaces for its animals, and would change its animal shows to address some of the concerns for the orcas' health and well-being.

in the same way that humans do. In 2002, the German *parliament* became the first in the world to vote that the right of animals to live free from exploitation should become part of the country's constitution.

In 1822, Britain became the first country to make a law covering the welfare of animals and followed it up with other laws protecting domestic, farmed, and captive animals. In the US, every state and the District of Columbia has laws against animal cruelty. Forty one states plus the District of Columbia can charge violators with a felony-level crime.

The Animal Welfare Act is a federal law that regulates animal research, shelters and pounds, transportation of animals, and stolen animals. It was first passed in 1966 and amended several times through 1996. One of the laws states that shelters must hold a dog or cat for at least five days for recovery by an owner or adoption before selling it to a dealer. Among many other laws are those covering the treatment of performing animals, pets, wild mammals, and working dogs.

Governments worldwide have joined forces to support the Bonn Convention, which aims to conserve land-based, marine, and flying migratory species.

 Words to Understand in This Chapter

extremist—a person who takes severe actions to promote a cause.

parliament—the group of people who are responsible for making the laws in certain types of government such as in the United Kingdom or Germany.

A friendly, intelligent dog is good company. Should he have the same rights as his owner?

The International Whaling Commission (IWC) used to govern how whales were hunted and killed. Now it's more concerned with protecting the survival of the world's largest mammals.

The International Whaling Commission (IWC) controls the extent to which whales can be killed for food and other products. Other organizations also protect a variety of wild species, but, as the World Society for the Protection of Animals (WSPA) points out, "there is still no government-level international forum at which animal welfare concerns are discussed and ruled upon," let alone one that considers the issue of their legal rights.

Are Views the Same Everywhere?

People's attitudes towards animals vary from country to country and depend on all sorts of things, especially wealth.

Many people today do not directly work on the land or with animals, but in some countries, people's chances of survival depend entirely on what they can grow or raise themselves. They may be too busy simply struggling to stay alive to worry

People in the twenty-first century can choose not to wear, eat or do anything that harms animals. There are plenty of alternatives.

How Can People Avoid Using Animals?

More and more people are realizing that they can make a difference by making small changes to the way they live.

- **What shall I eat?** Some people choose to eat meat and other foodstuffs that come from organically farmed animals that are humanely slaughtered. Others choose not to eat meat or use animal products at all.
- **What shall I buy?** People can decide not to buy clothes, shoes, bags, or other goods that are made from animal skins. They can buy cosmetics and household goods that have not been tested in ways that involve cruelty to animals.
- **What shall I do for entertainment?** People can choose not to go to circuses and zoos that keep animals in confined spaces or force them to behave in ways that are not natural to them. They can stop supporting sporting events that endanger animals in any way. There are plenty of alternative forms of entertainment, such as football games, bowling, and movies, which do not involve animals.
- **Can I avoid drugs tested on animals?** People who eat sensibly and get plenty of exercise tend to stay healthier than those who do not. They may be less likely to suffer from infections that need treatment with drugs tested on animals. Some medical practitioners offer treatments that help patients to avoid using drugs at all.

about animals. Those who have enough money can tell law-makers to protect animals and the land they live on from exploitation. A developing country's need to feed its starving people may mean it adopts intensive farming methods that use land and water more efficiently than traditional ones.

People in the USA, Canada, Australia, New Zealand, Europe, and South Africa can choose to use products like shampoo, laundry detergent, air fresheners, and toilet cleaners that are not tested on animals, but people in other countries may not have that choice. They may not have access to those products at all. A child in Africa, given life-saving drugs to deal with malaria or AIDS, may not be aware, and may not care, that the medicine has been tested on animals.

Animal Rights or Animal Welfare?

Some people who have no wish to see animals mistreated or exploited by humans say animals should only be used for human benefit if they are properly cared for. They believe it should be possible to farm animals and slaughter them for food in

Some cosmetics carry a label that says they haven't been tested on animals. Such labels can be misleading, as there is no legal legal definitions for these terms. Some of the raw products used in cosmetics were originally tested on animals to ensure they were safe. The company may justify its claim of being "cruelty free" because such testing is no longer needed.

Peaceful demonstrations make headlines and show governments how people feel about issues. These members of a farm animal rights group are taking part in the Global Climate March in Washington, D.C., on November 29, 2015.

ways that do not cause suffering. Laboratory animals used to test new products can be looked after well and not exposed to unnecessary pain. The welfare of animals kept for the purposes of sport, entertainment, and companionship can be protected by law.

Animal-rights campaigners say that people who support the right of humans to use animals for their own benefit are missing the point. They compare them to those people who used to regard other humans as their property, keeping them as slaves.

What Can I Do?

Societies are made up of individual people. Individuals all have the right to their own opinions and the right to express them. They have the right to influence other people as long as they do it within the law.

Whatever you think about animals and their rights, you can make a difference. You can find out as much as you can about

 Reasons Favoring Animal Research

- Animal research has helped to develop vaccines, antibiotics, and anesthetics used in all forms of surgery.
- Without animal research, there would have been no organ transplants, blood transfusions, replacement heart valves, or kidney dialysis.
- Medicines tested on or produced from animals can now overcome serious human conditions such as diabetes, asthma, and high blood pressure.
- Human illnesses such as cancer, heart disease, depression, and HIV are being treated by medicines tested on animals.
- Researchers are using animals to find treatments for conditions such as cystic fibrosis, Alzheimer's disease, stroke, spinal-cord damage, and malaria.

Source: Understanding Animal Research, www.understandinganimalresearch.org.uk/
about-us/science-action-network/forty-reasons-why-we-need-animals-in-research.

Animal-rights groups often enlist celebrities to help them get publicity. Actress Pamela Anderson has for many years been a prominent spokesperson for the American organization People for the Ethical Treatment of Animals (PETA).

the ways animals are treated by reading books, newspapers, and magazines, and websites.

Everyone can make up their own minds about what they think once they know the facts. Anyone can make lifestyle choices. If you decide that you are concerned about the way animals are treated, you can try to influence your family and friends to think and make lifestyle choices like you do, but remember that they all have the right to make up their own minds too!

Everyone has the right to join organizations and pressure groups that use legal means to change public opinion and influence the politicians who make laws. You will find the names and contact details of some influential organizations in the back of this book.

Anyone can support the work of their chosen organizations by giving money or time to help them do it. They can help organize or support fundraising events or give things they no longer need to charity shops that can make money by selling them.

Some people are good at writing letters to local newspapers about the work of animal charities and rescue centers in their area. Their letters or stories may be interesting enough to be printed and may influence other people to get involved.

Anyone who thinks animals in their neighborhood are being neglected or mistreated in some way can let someone know about it rather than standing back and doing nothing. The kind of person who can help might be a parent or teacher who can talk you through what you know and help you decide what to do next. If they agree that you are right to be concerned, you could contact a local animal charity or rescue center that can investigate further.

 # Text-Dependent Questions

1. What was the first country to make a law regarding the welfare of animals?
2. How does the Animal Welfare Act of 1966 protect animals' well-being?
3. What are three ways a person can promote animal welfare?

 # Research Project

Some people advocate for human welfare over animal welfare because millions of humans are starving, and they believe human survival and quality of life are the most important things. Others claim that animals do not have to be treated cruelly just so people can be comfortable. Using the Internet or your school library, do some research on the welfare of humans and animals, and answer the following question: "Is human welfare more important than animal welfare?" Write a two-page report, using data you have found in your research to support your conclusion, and present it to your class.

Appendix

Statistics on Global Animal Farming

The global livestock sector is growing faster than any other agricultural sub-sector, according to a report by the United Nations Food and Agricultural Organization (FAO). It provides livelihoods to about 1.3 billion people and contributes about 40 percent to global agricultural output. For many poor farmers in developing countries livestock are also a source of renewable energy for draft and an essential source of organic fertilizer for their crops.

But such rapid growth exacts a steep environmental price, according to the FAO report *Livestock's Long Shadow: Environmental Issues and Options*. "The environmental costs per unit of livestock production must be cut by one half, just to avoid the level of damage worsening beyond its present level," the report warns.

When emissions from land use and land use change are included, the livestock sector accounts for 9 percent of CO_2 deriving from human-related activities, but produces a much larger share of even more harmful greenhouse gases. It generates 65 percent of human-related nitrous oxide, which has 296 times the Global Warming Potential (GWP) of CO_2. Most of this comes from manure. And it accounts for 37 percent of all human-induced methane (23 times as warming as CO_2), which is largely produced by the digestive system of ruminants, and 64 percent of ammonia, which contributes significantly to acid rain.

Livestock now use 30 percent of the earth's entire land surface, mostly permanent pasture but also including 33 percent of the global arable land used to producing feed for livestock, the report notes. As forests are cleared to create new pastures, it is a major driver of deforestation, especially in Latin America where, for example, some 70 percent of former forests in the Amazon have been turned over to grazing.

Land and Water

At the same time herds cause wide-scale land degradation, with about 20 percent of pastures considered as degraded through overgrazing, compaction and erosion. This figure is even higher in the drylands where inappropriate policies and inadequate livestock management contribute to advancing desertification.

The livestock business is among the most damaging sectors to the earth's increasingly scarce water resources, contributing among other things to water pollution, eutrophication and the degeneration of coral reefs. The major polluting agents are animal wastes, antibiotics and hormones, chemicals from tanneries, fertilizers and the pesticides used to spray feed crops. Widespread overgrazing disturbs water cycles, reducing replenishment of above and below ground water resources. Significant amounts of water are withdrawn for the production of feed.

# Pet Statistics

The American Society for the Prevention of Cruelty to Animals estimated that in 2015 in the US:

- Approximately 7.6 million companion animals enter animal shelters nationwide every year. Of those, approximately 3.9 million are dogs, and 3.4 million are cats.
- Each year, approximately 2.7 million animals are euthanized (1.2 million dogs and 1.4 million cats).
- Approximately 2.7 million shelter animals are adopted each year (1.4 million dogs and 1.3 million cats).
- About 649,000 animals who enter shelters as strays are returned to their owners. Of those, 542,000 are dogs, and only 100,000 are cats.
- Of the dogs entering shelters, approximately 35 percent are adopted, 31 percent are euthanized, and 26 percent of dogs who came in as strays are returned to their owner.
- Of the cats entering shelters, approximately 37 percent are adopted, 41 percent are euthanized, and less than 5 percent of cats who came in as strays are returned to their owners.
- No one knows how many stray dogs and cats live in the United States; estimates for cats alone range up to 70 million.
- Only 10 percent of the animals received by shelters have been spayed or neutered, while 83 percent of pet dogs and 91 percent of pet cats are spayed or neutered.

Source: The American Society for the Prevention of Cruelty to Animals.

Livestock are estimated to be the main inland source of phosphorous and nitrogen contamination of the South China Sea, contributing to biodiversity loss in marine ecosystems.

Meat and dairy animals now account for about 20 percent of all terrestrial animal biomass. Livestock's presence in vast tracts of land and its demand for feed crops also contribute to biodiversity loss; 15 out of 24 important ecosystem services are assessed as in decline, with livestock identified as a culprit.

Facts about Livestock Farming

According to a 2014 article in the science journal *Nature*, "Close to one billion of the world's poorest people rely on livestock for their livelihood." According to the FAO, the greatest concentrations of livestock are found where there are the most people, including China (1.37 billion) India (1.28 billion), and Europe (750 million).

China farms half of the world's pigs and poultry (most poultry in China are ducks rather than chickens), and their numbers are increasing quickly.

India is the world's biggest milk producer, but industrialized countries are the most efficient milk producers. However, farmers in India and China can now produce milk, mutton, and pork almost as efficiently as industrialized countries can.

Livestock numbers are generally increasing worldwide, particularly those of pigs and chickens. However, some livestock numbers are falling. For example, the numbers of pigs and bovines (cattle) in most of Europe are lower now than they were forty years ago. The number of poultry in Scandinavia and eastern Europe is lower than it used to be. There are fewer sheep and goats in central Europe and the former Soviet Union. However, the falling numbers do not necessarily mean that less meat is being produced. Production methods are becoming more efficient, so fewer animals are required to yield the same amount of meat.

There are more sheep and goats than cattle in regions north of the tropics, in a band stretching from Spain and Libya to China. Goats are usually more common than sheep near the Equator. Developing countries are most efficient at producing meat and milk from sheep and goats.

Across the world, there is a move away from traditionally-farmed ruminant species (bovines, sheep and goats) towards more intensively-reared monogastric species (chickens and pigs). Ruminant species remain widespread in many less-developed regions and continue to be critically important to the rural poor.

Organizations
to Contact

Many animal-rights organizations produce written information that they will send to you or your school/college if you contact them. Some provide speakers who will talk to young people about the work they do.

Organizations in the United States

American Anti-Vivisection Society
801 Old York Road, Suite 204
Jenkintown, PA 19046-1611
Website: www.aavs.org

**American Society for the Prevention
of Cruelty to Animals (ASPCA)**
424 E. 92nd Street
New York, NY 10128-6804
Website: www.aspca.org

American Humane Association
1400 16th Street NW, Suite 360
Washington, DC 20036
Website: www.americanhumane.org

The Humane Society of the United States

2100 L Street, NW

Washington, D.C. 20037

Website: www.hsus.org

International Fund for Animal Welfare

1350 Connecticut Avenue NW, Suite 1220

Washington, DC 20036

Website: www.ifaw.org

National Association for Biomedical Research

1100 Vermont Avenue, NW, Suite 1100

Washington, DC 20005

Website: www.nabr.org

People for the Ethical Treatment of Animals (PETA)

501 Front Street

Norfolk, VA 23510

Website: www.peta.org

Animal Transportation Association (ATA)

PO Box 3363

Warrenton, VA 20188

Website: www.animaltransportationassociation.org

International Organizations

Humane Society International
2100 L Street, NW
Washington, D.C. 20037
Website: www.hsi.org

International Animal Rescue
Lime House
Regency Close
Uckfield, East Sussex
TN22 1DS United Kingdom
Website: www.internationalanimalrescue.org/

Birdlife International
Wellbrook Court, Girton Road
Cambridge
CB3 0NA United Kingdom
Website: www.birdlife.org

Compassion in World Farming
River Court, Mill Lane
Godalming, Surrey
GU7 1EZ United Kingdom
Website: www.ciwf.com

World Animal Protection

222 Grays Inn Road, 5th floor

London

WC1X 8HB United Kingdom

Website: www.worldanimalprotection.org

Series Glossary

apartheid—literally meaning "apartness," the political policies of the South African government from 1948 until the early 1990s designed to keep peoples segregated based on their color.

BCE and CE—alternatives to the traditional Western designation of calendar eras, which used the birth of Jesus as a dividing line. BCE stands for "Before the Common Era," and is equivalent to BC ("Before Christ"). Dates labeled CE, or "Common Era," are equivalent to *Anno Domini* (AD, or "the Year of Our Lord").

colony—a country or region ruled by another country.

democracy—a country in which the people can vote to choose those who govern them.

detention center—a place where people claiming asylum and refugee status are held while their case is investigated.

ethnic cleansing—an attempt to rid a country or region of a particular ethnic group. The term was first used to describe the attempt by Serb nationalists to rid Bosnia of Muslims.

house arrest—to be detained in your own home, rather than in prison, under the constant watch of police or other government forces, such as the army.

reformist—a person who wants to improve a country or an institution, such as the police force, by ridding it of abuses or faults.

republic—a country without a king or queen, such as the US.

United Nations—an international organization set up after the end of World War II to promote peace and co-operation throughout the world. Its predecessor was the League of Nations.

UN Security Council—the permanent committee of the United Nations that oversees its peacekeeping operations around the world.

World Bank—an international financial organization, connected to the United Nations. It is the largest source of financial aid to developing countries.

World War I—A war fought in Europe from 1914 to 1918, in which an alliance of nations that included Great Britain, France, Russia, Italy, and the United States defeated the alliance of Germany, Austria-Hungary, the Ottoman Empire, and Bulgaria.

World War II—A war fought in Europe, Africa, and Asia from 1939 to 1945, in which the Allied Powers (the United States, Great Britain, France, the Soviet Union, and China) worked together to defeat the Axis Powers (Germany, Italy, and Japan).

Further Reading

Baur, Gene. *Living the Farm Sanctuary Life: The Ultimate Guide to Eating Mindfully, Living Longer, and Feeling Better Every Day*. New York: Rodale, 2015.

Casey, Susan. *Voices in the Ocean: A Journey into the Wild and Haunting World of Dolphins*. New York: Doubleday, 2015.

Hargrove, John. *Beneath the Surface: Killer Whales, SeaWorld, and the Truth Beyond Blackfish*. New York: Palgrave, 2015.

Nance, Susan. *Entertaining Elephants: Animal Agency and the Business of the American Circus*. Baltimore: Johns Hopkins University Press, 2013.

Safina, Carl. *What Animals Think and Feel*. New York: Henry Holt and Co., 2015.

Fiction Books on Animal Rights Issues

George Orwell, *Animal Farm.*
This classic animals-take-over-the-farm story is an allegory about the origins and policies of the Soviet Union during the early twentieth century.

Anna Sewell, *Black Beauty.*
Fine, loyal horse endures suffering. First published in 1877 and instrumental in getting the use of the cruel bridle outlawed.

Henry Williamson, *Tarka the Otter.*
Life in the wild through an otter's eyes.

Michael Morpurgo, *The Butterfly Lion.*
A young boy rescues a white lion from the African bush.

Ernest Hemingway, *The Old Man and the Sea.*
Stirring story of an old fisherman's battle with his last big fish.

Richard Adams, *Watership Down*
Rabbits set out to find a new warren. Authentic account of animal behavior inside a gripping story—as much about freedom and human nature as it is about rabbits.

Internet Resources

www.friendsofanimals.org

Friends of Animals has facts and practical guides for wild and domesticated animals. It also has news and alerts for those who want the latest information on developing stories.

www.peta.org/blog

PETA's blog comments on issues of animal cruelty in association with Hollywood and the entertainment industry, especially concerning fashion.

www.cok.net

A US-based animal-rights group founded in the 1990s, Compassion over Killing campaigns for "a kinder life for all." It has a useful FAQ section on the thinking behind the animal-rights movement.

www.kids4research.org

This website explains how and why animals are used in research. It takes the view that animal experimentation may not be desirable—and one day may not be necessary at all—but that currently, it is the only way of getting the information scientists need to develop drugs and other products that are safe for humans, animals, and the environment.

www.animallaw.info

Michigan State University College of Law Animal Legal & Historical Center: A comprehensive storehouse of information about animal law, including over 1200 full text cases (US, historical, and UK), over 1400 US statutes, over 60 topics and comprehensive explanations, legal articles on a variety of animal topics, and an international collection.

Publisher's Note: The websites listed on these pages were active at the time of publication. The publisher is not responsible for websites that have changed their address or discontinued operation since the date of publication. The publisher reviews and updates the websites each time the book is reprinted.

Index

Numbers in **bold italics** refer to captions.